YOUR WORD IS NEAR

YOUR
WORD
IS
NEAR

Contemporary Christian Prayers

HUUB OOSTERHUIS

translated by N. D. Smith

PAULIST PRESS

New York, N.Y.   Paramus, N.J.

A Paulist Press Edition, originally published under the title *Bid om Vrede* by Uitgeverij Ambo N.V., Utrecht, Netherlands, 1966.

Copyright © 1968 by
The Missionary Society
of St. Paul the Apostle
in the State of New York

Library of Congress
Catalog Card Number: 68-20848

ISBN 0-8091-1775-4

Published by Paulist Press
Editorial Office: 1865 Broadway, N.Y., N.Y. 10023
Business Office: Paramus, N.J. 07652

Printed and bound in the
United States of America

CONTENTS

*Prayers of petition

THE SON OF MEN

Prayers for Lent
about Jesus in the hands of men
about God and his silence
in fear and impotence
for this world, for redemption

*Prayers of petition

FIRE IN OUR MOUTHS

BREAD IN HIS HANDS

stones for bread?
for God's presence
beyond the frontiers

GREATER THAN OUR HEARTS

Sin and guilt
for forgiveness and a new beginning

HERE IN OUR MIDST

about the city of God

a world fit for men to live in
that we may see
for a new future
God of Jesus, my God

*Prayers of petition

SUGGESTIONS FOR USE

This book is not primarily intended to be read straight through from cover to cover. It has a structure, and the various texts have been arranged with some care in the form of a developing idea, a questing faith. It is a book to be read through at random, a book that may provide the point of departure for personal prayer, for meditation and silence.

It is, moreover, a book for the liturgy. Almost all the prayers in this book have been tried out from week to week in practice. Most of them were written to be spoken aloud and, what is more, to be spoken at a definite moment in the celebration of the eucharist.

The following can be used as opening prayers or collects: the prayers on pages 17-23, 27-29, 47, 66, 104-107, 116, 149-151, 159.

The following can be used as concluding prayers or postcommunions: pages 34 (first prayer), 50 (second prayer), 51 (first prayer), 73, 108, 137 (second prayer), 139-140, 140 (second prayer), 151 (second prayer).

Specific opening and closing prayers for every Sunday in the liturgical year will not be found in this book. Many of the texts can be used on more than one Sunday. Frequently, however, the prayers are attuned to the scriptural readings given in the Roman Missal for a particular Sunday. The reader will discover this for himself. A few suggestions are given here:

1st Sunday of Advent:
    Your word is near 17
3rd Sunday of Advent:
    How many times, God 19

The prayers of petition are listed as such in the contents or are indicated by asterisks. All the prayers in this book are offered simply as "models," and whoever is leading the liturgy can choose from these models the formulas most useful to him, adapting them to the constantly changing situation.

On pages 130-134 the reader will find a specimen English canon. The original Dutch translation of the *Sanctus* was made in collaboration with the Rev. Dr. W. Barnard.

INTRODUCTION

Prayer is naive. It is waiting for someone who never
comes, asking and asking for someone or something
that is not there.

If there is a God who loves man,
let him speak *now*. Now.

The Latin poet Seneca put this into the mouths of the
chorus in his tragedy *Thyestes*.

I echo him:

"If there is a God present here,
let him answer me. Now."

No reply. No one gets up, and perhaps that's
a good thing.

Prayer is monotonous. Always the same words.
Constant variations on the same theme—have mercy
on us, be merciful to us, take pity on us. The whole of
world literature and every song is simply a variation
on that one theme, the theme of love and death and pity.

There is very little that we have to say and think.
But we *can* vary this one theme, give it different shades
of meaning in endless repetitions. The medieval story
of Tristan and Isolde began with the words, "Will you
hear about love and death." And even now, we still
go on varying this sentence in different keys. Praying
also is playing variations on a familiar theme—be
merciful to us, be present here, what is your name.

People pray to each other. The way I say "you"
to someone else, respectfully, intimately, desperately.
The way someone says "you" to me, hopefully,
expectantly, intensely, his voice seeking or caressing.
It may be that praying to God grew out of this
human way of speaking to each other.

We know nothing about the origin of the phenomenon
we call "prayer." Where did we get it from? How did
mankind come by it? Praying is simply there as a
matter of course, in all the holy books of all the
religions of mankind. It is simply there—it came
suddenly, perhaps, or else it just always has been there.

Prayer is simply a matter of course in the bible.
It was so much taken for granted that, to begin with,
Israel had no word for "pray." The word for praying
was rejoicing, laughing, crying, reviling, imploring,
according to how one felt.

There were hardly any fixed rites, specially privileged
places, or strictly prescribed times for prayer in Israel.
Everything was allowed—that was the most powerful
impulse in this people's relationship with their God.
There was no special language for prayer, sacred and
sublime. You could pray in every posture and every
mode. The God of Israel was quite different from

all other gods. He was not a god who compelled, made demands and used force. He was not a "mother earth and father heaven" to whom men had to bear sacrifices with their backs bent, not a god who had to be addressed with lowered gaze and muted tongues in a standardized jargon, a language that was consciously experienced as simple and artless or as formal. The God of Israel was space and freedom, and you could say anything to him. No word was too uncouth or too spontaneous to be used with him. He was, after all, the one with whom Abraham, the father of that people, argued about Sodom and Gomorrah.

God is the one to whom you can speak as the man Job spoke. Praying is what Job is doing in the following fragment:

Job raised his eyes and called to heaven:
I will not keep my mouth shut.
I must express the bitterness of my soul—
    you force me to it.
Am I the sea, or a sea monster, perhaps,
    to be locked up and guarded by you?
There is no comfort for me, even when I am in bed—
    you come to scare me with dreams
    with visions of terror.
I would rather be strangled.
What is man, that you are so interested in him,
    that you give him such attention,
    that you look every morning to see if he is still there,
    that you test him every moment?
When at last will you look away from me,
    or let me alone till I swallow my spittle?

What have I done to you, prying watcher of men?
Why have you made me your target?
And why am I a burden to you?
Why can't you forget about my sin?
Why don't you overlook my shortcomings?
Soon I shall lie down in the dust—
    then you may look for me,
    but I shall not be there any more.

It was in this world of the God of Abraham and Job that Jesus of Nazareth lived.

Christians should turn back again and again to the words of Jesus of Nazareth to learn how to pray.

How did Jesus pray? The gospel tells us that men began to doubt their own prayer when they saw him praying. "Teach us to pray," they asked him and his answer was, "Our Father, who art in heaven, hallowed be thy name. . . ." In another place, we are told that he prayed the psalms—"God, my God, why have you forsaken me?"

The psalms are everything that is in man. Memories, ideas, feelings of every kind collide and crash against each other in the psalms, in a constant altercation between God and no God.

What is man that you remember him,
    the son of Adam that you care for him?

says psalm 8, and psalm 22 says:

I cry by day: my God, and you are silent—
I cry by night and you just let me.

Again,

> You have been, O Lord, a safe dwelling place
>> for us from generation to generation

and right next to it, in the same psalm (90), jolting
and bumping:

> You make people turn to dust.
> You say: it's all over, O children of Adam.

The world of the psalms is the world in which Jesus
lived—the world of psalm 42:

> As a hart stretches out for living water,
>> so do I reach out, God, with all my being toward you.
> I thirst for God, for the living God.
> When shall I at last stand face to face with God? . . .
> Why do I go about tearing my clothes,
>> tormented and humiliated?
> My enemies scare me to death,
>> mortally wounding my body.
> Where is that God of yours, I hear them call.
> You are my rescuer,
> You are my God.

All this and more is contained in psalm 42, that
nervous, neurotic poem full of inner conflict, for and
against. It is a prayer that opens passionately, then sinks
into inner doubt, then blazes up in a vision of almost
cosmic fear and at last finds peace and tranquillity.
The spirit is gradually purified in this violent

movement and the last, tentative word is reached:
"You are my God."

Praying, we shall have to turn more and more toward
the psalms. In our liturgical prayer, too, we must try
to sound the depths of the psalms and match their
quality, evoking for each other the world of
Israel's prayer.

I have tried to do this in *Your Word Is Near*, for
example, in the litany of the "names of God" at the end
of the book. I have tried to tell the name of God as a
story, a recitative of men's names and facts, ending with a
variation on that word of psalm 42, "You are my God."

God of me
tongue of snow
and of rapture
voice that catches
in my throat
storm-wind head-wind
covering me
tender rigid
like a body.
God of no one
simply people
march of ages
stranger we come
slowly to know
you elusive
stone of the sages
you not God
as we think you
furnace of silence
difficult friend.

Praying is speaking God's name, or rather, seeking God's name. "What is your name?"—the eternal question that comes back again after every answer. It is the question asked by Moses who was permitted to meet God as a "difficult friend" and to talk with him "as a man talks with his friend." The question is given to this book as a motto.

Praying is trying to turn that little word "God" into a name that means something to me, to us, now. It is trying to make that hazardous, volatile little word really expressive. You get nowhere if you just say "God." Those three letters—they are just a code, an unknown quantity, a stopgap. You have to make the long journey from "God," a meaningless, boring, empty cliché, to "our God," "my God," "God of the living," a meaningful, personal name full of echoes of his entire history with mankind, if you really want to pray.

God, this word we call you by
is almost dead and meaningless,
transient and empty
like all the words men use.
We ask you
to renew its force and meaning,
to make it once again
a name that brings your promise to us.
Make it a living word
which tells us
that you will be for us
as you have always been—
trustworthy and hidden
and very close to us,
our God, now and for ever.

A name is not just a word. A person's name is full of history. A person's name—it at once calls to mind facts and experiences, joy and sorrow, misunderstandings. Speaking a friend's name—it reminds me at once of what we have in common, of the depth and the height of our whole relationship, our life together. I have heard people say of a dead person, "When I speak his name, then he really *is* there."

Calling someone by his name. It is giving him the chance to be himself, to become conscious of himself. It is taking him seriously. If you never call a person by his name, you can humiliate him, isolate him. Even worse—you are in fact taking away his status as a man if you never speak his name, never address him by his first name, but always make do with his surname or a nickname or some corruption of his real name, or if you just call out to him.

Praying is "blessing," "praising," "giving honor to" God. That is what the psalms call it. Calling God by his name, giving him the chance to be himself, "our God." In psalm 104, the psalmist begins by naming God:

I will call you, God, by your name
as truly as I am alive

and then goes on to talk about creation. He drags everything in, going right back to the beginning, when

the waters were still above the mountains

and then we have wild goats leaping in the hills and the grass and plants growing in the fields and then— man, toiling until darkness falls. Swaggering about the

8

whole world like this, the psalmist hits on the track of God's name:

> All this, God, your very own work—
> your wisdom speaks from so many things,
> our earth is full of your power of creation.

Who is God? What is his name? He is what he does to us. He is called "our earth is full of his power of creation." When the bible prays, the whole of creation is listed and the whole of God's history with man is brought up again. When we pray, with the bible, we appeal to creation and to the covenant. We call God to mind and remind him who he is and what he has done. What God used to mean for men in the past includes a promise of the future, the promise that he will mean something for us as well, that he will be someone for us.

Theology has called this kind of prayer *anamnēsis*, recalling, remembering, speaking again what God has done, recollecting who he is, reciting his *facta et gesta*. It is, after all, only very gradually, throughout the course of a human history and through the medium of human forms, that God makes himself known to us.

You who called Abraham to leave his own little world and made him fruitful, you who gave Moses your name and led him in one piece through the sea and the desert, you who took David away from his sheep, you who gave your saving power its full force in Jesus, whom you redeemed from death—you are quite welcome to do as you like with us too, our God.

This structure can be recognized in the eucharistic prayer at the Lord's table, which is an outstanding example of *anamnēsis*. Celebrating the eucharist is also keeping God to his word, and his word is Jesus:

Your beloved son,
whom you called and sent
to serve us and give us light . . .
the likeness and the form
of your constant love and goodness . . .
this unforgettable man
who has fulfilled everything
that is human—
our life and death . . .
[who] gave himself,
heart and soul, to this world . . .
[who] on the night that he was delivered up,
took bread into his hands . . .

The intercessions, or "prayers of petition," are also essentially a form of *anamnēsis*. We look around us in our own world today and listen to its voices, almost lost in its vastness, and enumerate our cares and worries again and again, speaking about them as persistently as the newspapers do. We particularize our needs in the prayers of petition, so that, within the congregation, they are a proclamation of our existence as human beings. They also call upon us to understand, to extend our frontiers. As the Dutch poet Simon Vinkenoog has put it, "praying is coming to share a greater inward space."

The prayers of petition tell us—this world is your horizon, Vietnam is part of you, war—we ourselves are war, sick, lonely and dead people—we are sick, lonely and dead, I am that man.

Let us pray
for all who have to live with injustice,
who are caught up in an inhuman system
and who cannot make any headway under it.
For all soldiers at the front
who have to fight and kill
against their will and against their consciences.

Let us pray
for all who have lost heart
because of so much evil in the world.
But also for those who are optimistic,
for those who radiate strength
and can offer friendship—
that they may not fail when they are tested
and that we may never lack their companionship.

Interceding is praying for others, being aware of
them, recognizing them, wanting to be bound up with
them, wanting to support them and bear their burdens
and yet still daring to let them go out of your hands.

So concerned with our world, with its people,
we say: "You are concerned with all this, God. You
are concerned with everything to do with us. You
were not ashamed to be called our God."

Again and again, prayer is not knowing who
God is, calling him by weak and questionable names.
But he is not our names, our words. He is not as
we think he is.

Is he great, sublime? In the history of prayer,
in that aspect of the Church's life and history that is

most hidden and most difficult to grasp, there have always been people who were convinced that, for the God of Jesus of Nazareth, the least of men, all great words were far too great. They dared to speak of the foolishness of God—he is humble, he is nobody, he went the way of all seed, dying and getting nowhere. Is God the light—is he the broad light of day? No, he is darkness, deep night, the void. He is not a lofty tree, but a shapeless twig, not the vast sea, but a glass of water, not a powerful voice, but a vulnerable silence.

That is what we experience in prayer also. We know the folly of God. We know that we cannot grasp him, that he is incalculable, defenseless, and different, that he is no answer and solves nothing, that he is no good to us; misery is still misery, we are no better off because of him—and yet. . . . Just like a man who has a friend—that solves nothing at all, dead is still dead. And yet . . .

This experience is the background to the prayer, the song:

> You are no answer God
> to all our questions
> you are no comfort to us
> when at our utmost limit
> all life seems pointless
> and we can go no farther . . .
> You do not fill in gaps . . .
> You are no law God
> and no first principle . . .
> You are the defendant
> without defense . . .

You are not everything
you say so little.

Praying is a way of living, of waiting, keeping the
door open, not having, asking. Praying is pleading
for things, for people, for everything that is ordinary—
not compelling, not seizing hold of reality or forcing
it to reveal itself, but asking.

Let us pray
for everything that is ordinary—
for food and drink every day,
for clothes to wear,
for a safe journey . . .
for the light of our eyes . . .
for the sympathy and affection
of our fellow men.

It is what was known in the past as the "spiritual
life." Not living from what you have, what you possess,
but from what can still become, from hope, from the
wind. Paul called this attitude *faith*, saying "and
yet . . ." And yet can become what is not yet.
Peace in Vietnam, for example.

We cannot, all of us, make peace in Vietnam come
true. We still cannot—we are caught up in schemes,
the need for an armament industry linked to the
economic process, the balance of power in Southeast
Asia, all those gods, all those sticks to beat us with.
But we try to believe that God is greater than schemes,
that he is the Lord of all powers and gods.

Sometimes I think that demonstrating for peace in

Vietnam, doing something concrete like joining in a march, really has something to do with faith and with prayer. Maybe this sort of protest is a desperate attempt to keep the case open everywhere in the world. Somewhere, a thousand or so people who don't know what to God they ought to do just begin to walk in order to show that it could be different, that we, a bunch of people, a thousand or so marching, are greater and more eternal than the war.

There are people who feel this way about it; protest is born in them. They are the poor in spirit. All appearance and all reason is against them. What sort of influence can their marching have, in God's name, on events in the world? Well, precisely the same influence as prayer, I think. When we pray in the liturgy, together with others in our congregations, for peace, we associate ourselves with this kind of fruitless demonstration. Appearances and reason are against us, too—what happens to prayer like that? But just imagine if we were to give up asking for peace, just like that, desperately or naively? We would probably become choked up ourselves, shut up like clams. So we say, let us pray. We keep the door open to the possibility of peace, of a new creation. We open our minds to the possibility that it *is* something—grace.

Huub Oosterhuis

YOUR WORD IS NEAR

What shall I say to them
if they ask me,
what is his name?

Exodus 3, 13

✠ You wait for us
until we are open to you.
We wait for your word
to make us receptive.
Attune us to your voice,
to your silence,
speak and bring your son to us—
Jesus, the word of your peace.

✠ Your word is near,
O Lord our God,
your grace is near.
Come to us, then,
with mildness and power.
Do not let us be deaf to you,
but make us receptive and open
to Jesus Christ your son,
who will come to look for us and save us
today and every day
for ever and ever.

✠ You, God, arouse faith in our hearts,
whoever we are.
You know and accept all your people,
whatever their thoughts are of you.
Speak to the world, then, your word,
come with your heaven among us,
give to good and to bad men your sun,
for ever and ever.

+ Grant us, O Lord,
a sign of life,
show us, O God,
how much we mean to you.
Come into our world
with your word of creation.
Make us fit to receive you
and grant us your peace.

+ Sow freely, Lord God,
the seed of your word over the world.
May it fall in good soil in us
and may it be heard
wherever men live.

+ Do not turn from us, God,
and do not avoid us
now that we are looking
for words to pray to you.
For if we call you God
and speak your name
we do so because you have promised
that you will not be far from all
who call upon you.

+ Hear us, O Lord,
we implore you,
for who is to be our salvation
if you do not take us to heart?
Subdue the powers
that seek our lives
and give us hope
for the sake of him
who has conquered death—
Christ, your son,
who lives with you
in the fellowship of the Holy Spirit
for ever and ever.

+ How many times, God,
have we been told
that you are no stranger,
remote from those who call upon you
in prayer!
O let us see, God,
and know in our lives now
that those words are true.
Give us faith
and give us the joy
of recognizing your son,
Jesus Christ,
our savior, in our midst.

+ Make us receptive and open,
and may we accept your kingdom
like children taking bread
from the hands of their father.
Let us live in your peace,
at home with you
all the days of our lives.

+ Lord God,
your constant love of man
has been handed down
in human words to us.
In this way you are our God and father.
We pray
that we may eagerly listen
to the words of your gospel
and in this way be with you heart and soul
in the fellowship of the Holy Spirit.

+ How can you want us
to fall, God, and not
to get up again?
How can you want us
to stray and not
to find rest?
Do not let us be caught
in a web of confusion,
but send out your light
and your faithfulness to meet us,
send us your son,
Jesus Christ,
your care for this world.

✠ O Lord, our God,
you give your light, your word
to all who want it.
You give your kingdom
to the poor and the sinners.
Then why not give us too
your grace.
Do not send us away
emptyhanded,
but fill us with your son,
your word, the light
and life of the world
for all ages.

✠ We can expect nothing, God,
from ourselves
and everything that we have
comes from you.
We are dependent on your love
and your kindness.
Treat us well—
do not measure out your grace,
but give us your own power of life,
your son Jesus Christ,
mercy and faithfulness
more than we can imagine
today and all the days
of our lives.

✝ We are the work of your hands, O God.
You, Lord, have made us and love us.
All our life is your gift,
all your power was in
our creation
and thus you will go on giving to us
grace upon grace.
What more need we hope for
from you?
This certainty—God—
is good enough for us.

✝ God, you are merciful to us
in all our doings, good and bad.
You do not insist on your right
but acquit us
and accept us—
everything is possible with you.
Give us the spirit
to follow you,
make us merciful to each other
so that the world may know
who you are:
nothing but love, our father,
God.

✝ You watch over your creation,
a shepherd
with whom all living things are safe.
You know us all
and keep us
wherever we move.
O God, do this,
we ask you,
all the days of our lives—
may we never want
and may we enter your rest
and know your peace.
Today and every day
of our lives.

God, you are everywhere
present invisibile
near to us speaking—
the silence awaits you
mankind exists for you
men see and know you.

Men made of flesh and bone
men of light and of stone
men of hard stone and blood
a flow unstaunchable
mankind your people
your city on earth.

Earth is all that we are
dust is all that we make,
breathe into us, open us,
make us your earth
your heaven new made
your peace upon earth.

HEARING AND SEEING

The kingdom of God is
as if a man should scatter seed
upon the ground,
and should sleep and rise
night and day,
and the seed
should sprout and grow,
he knows not how.

Mark 4, 26

+ Why, God, are we divided,
why are we broken?
Can you not cure and save us
as you saved our brother
Jesus from the power of death?
We call upon you with him—
make us whole again
and restore us in honor,
renew the shape of this world
against every sin
and cover us with your light,
your Holy Spirit.
Make us immortal
today
and all the days of our lives.

+ Lord, our God, our happiness
is your concern.
Your glory it is
that our concern should be
to live happily as men.
May we see at last
this world cured, restored,
your name hallowed among us,
peace on earth
and may we see this come about
for the sake of him
who lives with you,
Jesus our Lord.

+ It is your word,
it is Jesus Christ
that we are aiming at, Lord God.
Whom else should we
expect from you?
He is your heart, your son,
your pity,
he is your eyes and has seen us,
he is your mouth and speaks to us
and we know and receive you
in his words.
We ask you, Lord,
to let us see this man,
knowing that who sees him
beholds you, the father,
and this is enough
for us as for this world
and for all times. Amen.

+ God,
you have sent the light
of your life to all men
to give them the grace
of the light of faith
so that they may have life
and have it abundantly.
We pray that you
will open our eyes to Christ
in whom you have made manifest
your love of men.
He is a word of light,
the way to life for every man
who lives in this world.
He is the son who lives
with you for all eternity.

+ *Prayers of petition*

Lord, our God,
in the name of all who live on earth
and with Jesus Christ, your son,
and in his Spirit,
we commend to you
our whole world,
all countries, races,
nations and people,
both young and old,
rich and poor.

In prayer to you we remember
all those who have gone before us,
all those who have preceded us into death,
all those from whom
we have inherited this world.
We pray for those
who have left us so many treasures and ruins,
so much love and sorrow.
We thank you
for our parents and ancestors,
for all who have made us what we are
and who have given us our names
and our language to speak
and our country to live in.

You are the God of our fathers
and have entrusted us with the task
of handing on life on earth
and in your own good time
you will reap what we have sown.
We ask you then:
bless our bodies so that we
may pass on life whole and entire
and bless our hands and minds
so that we do not build a world
that is alien from you.

We pray
for our children and our children's children,
for all who will be born after us,
that we do not give them stones
instead of bread,
that we do not leave them war,
but freedom, happiness and peace.

We pray to you
for all who are living now,
for all our fellow men,
for those who live in our town,
for those who share our home,
for our neighbors and acquaintances
and for everyone we know,
for our good friends.
We also try to pray, God,
for those for whom we feel no sympathy,
for those whom we avoid,
for those we cannot love,
for our enemies.

But above all we thank you
for those whom we love
and who make this world meaningful to us,
for the one who is closest to us,
as close as our own body,
our husband, our wife,
our children and all those
who have been given and entrusted to us.

We name those, Lord,
for whom we are deeply concerned,
for you know them all by name.
We pray for—
who has asked us to pray for him.
We pray for—
who is dying, and ask you
to sustain his faith in these moments.
We pray for—
who has died, and ask you
to give him peace,
now that all is consummated.

O Lord,
you are not a God of dead,
but of living people.
We ask you who have made us
to bless us
and keep us alive.
Receive us when we die,
renew us when we grow old,
make us open if we become closed to you,
for Jesus Christ's sake. Amen.

+ Do not let us continue, God,
to rely on our own powers
and do not allow us
to follow the wrong path,
but let your Spirit
have power over us
and put us on the path
that leads to peace,
through Jesus, the Messiah,
your word, our guide,
who lives and reigns with you.

+ You, God, are the heart
and truth of our life.
We ought to set no limit
to our search for your kingdom.
Give us the strength to continue
and not to turn from you
and not to refuse to accept you
when you come.
Give us the strength to do
as Jesus our brother did,
giving and losing himself
with heart and soul
to gain you,
our father and our God,
for this world and for all ages.

✛ You nourish and sustain the world
from day to day
and wherever we go
you are present more fully
than we dare presume.
We thank you for this presence,
this hidden, vulnerable,
yet faithful presence here and now.
We believe in it and live from you
as we live from bread
as we hunger and thirst
for peace.

✛ You are not indifferent, God,
to our joy and suffering.
Your deepest care is
for our lives and happiness.
Our peace is your peace.
We thank you
that you are so vulnerable
in all your people.
We pray to you,
let us grow
in this new and eternal covenant
as long as we live
for ever and ever.

+ By your word, Lord God,
you set free every man
imprisoned in himself.
To freedom you have called us
and to become men
in the image and the spirit
of Jesus Christ.
We beseech you,
give us the strength
that his life has first provided,
give us the openness
that he has prepared for us,
make us receptive and free
so that, with you,
we may live for this world.

+ We thank you, God, our grace,
for being alive, tomorrow and today,
for this earth, for bread and light,
for the people around us,
today, yesterday and every day.
We thank you for our lives
here and now, lives
laborious and full of joy.
And may neither future nor death
separate us from Jesus Christ,
who is your love for all mankind
and all the earth.

I believe in the living God,
father of Jesus Christ our Lord,
our God, our almighty father.

He has created the world, all things
in his only beloved son,
the image and likeness of his glory.

Jesus, light of eternal light,
word of God, faithful, abiding,
Jesus Christ, our grace and our truth.

In order to serve this world of ours,
in order to share our human lot,
he became flesh of our human flesh.

By the will of the Holy Spirit
and born of the virgin Mary
he became man, a man like us.

He was broken for our sins
and was obedient unto death
and gave himself upon the cross.

Therefore he has received the name
of the firstborn from the dead,
the son of God and Lord of all.

He will come in God's own time
to do justice to the living and the dead.
He is the man whom I shall resemble.

I believe in the power of the Spirit,
in the love of the father and the son
in the covenant of God with men,

in the Church, the body of Christ,
called together and sent forth
to do the work that he has done—

to enlighten and to serve
and to bear the sins of the world
and to build up peace on earth.

I believe that we shall arise
from death with a new, undying body,
for he is the God of the living.

Amen. Come, Lord Jesus, come.

+ *Prayers of petition*

You have awakened faith in us, God, you have spoken
the word of your gospel to us. You have happened
to us, God. We are no longer sure of ourselves and
of this world, and we hesitate to respond to you. We ask
you, God, to keep all these words in your heart.

Make us poor in spirit, God, unselfish and ready to
receive you. Make us sincere and pure in heart so that

we may recognize the signs of your presence. Let us
hunger for peace and thirst for justice and righteousness.
Make us gentle and forgiving. And be yourself
merciful to us. Teach us to pardon each other and
give us the strength to bear the suffering of others.

We pray for those who mourn and are in distress.
For the crippled, the infirm, the sick and the dying.
We pray for all who are disillusioned by life—for
married couples who have not been able to hold on to
each other, for parents who are disappointed in their
children.

We pray for those who have not met with happiness,
for all who have not found a partner in life and have
found no response to their longings and affections.

We pray, Lord, for the world today and especially
for all those who have been broken or disabled by war
or whose lives have been thrown into disorder by cruelty
or loneliness. We pray for all nations who are exploited,
for all who are poor and without legal rights, for all
who are despised and maltreated because of the color
of their skin.

We pray not only for all who have to suffer this
injustice, but also for those who foster and increase it.

We pray, Lord, for all who are deprived and have to
live in poverty. We pray for the millions of poor people
in India and elsewhere, for all the countries that are
overpopulated, for all our fellow men who live in

slums or in refugee camps, for all who are imprisoned
in their underworld. Give us the strength and call
people from among us to combat this poverty. Send
your Holy Spirit, who is light and wisdom and who
gives life, among us to enable us to find a way to exile
hunger and end war in our world.

You have given us life. Make us ready now to share it
with others so that our happiness may be as great as
our welfare. Protect us against our own hardness of
heart. Keep us open. In this way we will try to be your
Church, your chosen people, created and nourished by
you, known to you and receiving grace from you as one
body, your son on earth for ever and ever.

+ The faith of man, Lord God, is
irresistible to you.
And you give in
whenever they approach you
openly and sincerely
and appeal to you.
We call on you just as we are
and want you to do for us
whatever we ask of you.
Open your hand, God,
and give us all we need.
Give us what is good for us—
bread and peace,
the body of your son,
today and all the days
of our lives.

+ Let our world
have your blessing, God.
Remain with us
no matter what may happen.
Give us from your hand
our lives with all
its cares and pleasures.
And we hope
for a life of happiness
in this world
and in the world to come.

+ *For everything that is ordinary*

Let us pray
and never cease to ask
for everything we long for,
for everything we think we need,
let us pray that God
will give it to us.
For food and drink every day,
for clothes to wear,
for good health,
for a safe journey
throughout life,
and for every man
a home.

Let us pray
for the light of our eyes,
for the air we breathe,
for the voice we speak with,
for the sun and the rain in their seasons,
for plants and all creatures
that they may grow and prosper.
Let us pray
for all the things
we take for granted,
for everything that comes to us all the time
from God, our creator and our father.

And we also pray
for what we need most of all—
the sympathy and affection
of our fellow men,
for the faithfulness of friends,
for the faithfulness of God,
for the generosity
of those we have offended,
for the love of those we love.
Let us pray
for a safe future for our children,
for happy days and for our old people,
for pleasure in our work,
for patience in adversity,
for peace on earth.

For all those who lack
the most vital necessities
we would like to pray.
For health for those who are ill.
For new opportunities
for those who have failed.
For confidence and energy
for those who are disappointed.
Let us pray
that those who are lost
may meet with friendship
and those who are ill-used
and in poverty
may meet with justice.

And let us pray
that we too may do what is right
and choose truth rather than falsehood,
that we do not fail our fellow men
to further our own advantage,
that we do not call evil what is good,
that we do not speak ill of each other
and scoff at our neighbor.

To him who knows what we need
even before we ask him
we pray—
Lord our God,
accept our prayers
and make us receptive
to everything you can give us,
through Jesus Christ our Lord.

+ You are no answer God
to all our questions
you are no comfort to us
when at our utmost limit
all life seems pointless
and we can go no farther.
You are no refuge God
for all our ignorance
you do not fill in gaps—
no way to happiness
no source of welfare.
You are no law God
and no first principle
you bring no actions
are not all-knowing
you are not pure
you are not blameless
you the defendant
without defense.
You let life drift
and take its course
you are not here
not there not everywhere
you are not everything
you say so little.

NO OTHER SIGN

Jesus asked him,
Do you see anything?
The blind man looked up
and said,
I see men
but they look like trees
walking.

Mark 8, 23-24

⁺ You know us all, O God,
each one of us by name.
We are important to you,
each one of us is written
on the palms of your hands.
Now let us know as well,
God, your name,
know and feel it
in our hearts and lives—the name
that you have made known
and loved in Christ.

⁺ O God, your name
has been with us on earth
from the beginning,
a word so full of promise
that it has kept us going.
But in Jesus' life and death
you have revealed your name.
You, our father, can be found
in him for all time.
He is your word and promise
completely.
We ask you that we may
be drawn to him
and thereby come
to know you more and more.

+ *A Christmas carol*

In deepest night the star of morning
has heralded the infant's birth.
His coming is for us the dawning
of God's salvation here on earth.
Trust what you see, believe the vision,
lay bare your hearts to God's own word,
do not refuse the savior's mission,
accept the message you have heard.

God has no other sign, no other
light in our darkened world to give
than this man Christ to be our brother,
a God with whom we all can live.
He has revealed to every nation
his love of man in Christ our Lord.
In him all flesh may see salvation,
and earth made new in God's own word.

The promised one of Israel's story,
a bridegroom clad in fire and light,
the morning sun in all its glory
dispelling darkness and the night,
has come to dwell with us for ever,
uniting us in peace and love,
and in his body we need never
be parted from our God above.

+ Lord God and father of Jesus Christ
this is the night when he was born,
our hope and our salvation.
We pray to you
to let his light shine in our lives,
may we love him and keep him,
your word among us,
your peace on earth,
today and every day,
world without end.

+ Lord our God,
we celebrate this night
the birth of Jesus,
your son our Lord,
light of the world.
We ask you
to let us see in him
your grace and goodness
and that his light
may shine forth
now and always.

✝ Lord God,
this is the day that you have made
light of your light,
a day of great joy.
Reveal yourself to all
who grope in darkness,
come to those who mourn.
Let us see the light
that comforts us,
the kindly light,
and hear your good news
for this world for ever and ever.

✝ Father of Jesus Christ, our God,
confirm and strengthen our belief
that it is he whom we expect
and that your light
has shone in him
upon the world.
We pray to you,
take from us everything
that cannot bear this light
and make us love your peace.
Amen.

+ History has been made
among us by your name.
In receiving Jesus Christ your son
we have come to know you.
We ask you
to let this name stay with us,
may your word do its work
in every part of our being,
may your son grow among us,
a man of peace, for ever.

+ Your heart goes out
to insignificant and little things,
to children, to the poor—
these are your kingdom.
For you became yourself
defenseless and humble,
resembling a human word,
a piece of bread, a name
that has to die.
We ask you then,
let us resemble you,
let us, imperfect as we are,
become your children,
your own beloved son.

Let us pray
for all people of all ages,
for all who, young and old,
belong to each other
and go through life together.
Let us pray
that we may care for
and respect each other,
that we may not be divided,
but may with one mind try
to achieve happiness.

Let us pray
for all children,
for all among us who
are defenseless and small—
for a happy childhood.
Let us pray
that nothing may harm them,
that their lives may not become
distorted and perverse,
that we do not give them scandal
or teach them to hate,
but that we may lead them
to know the truth,
that we may have the courage
to protect the vulnerable,
the immature, the inexperienced
among us.

Let us pray
for our young people
whose lives lie ahead of them,
that they may go forward
with open and receptive minds
to meet their future,
that they may learn to live
with life's uncertainties
and face up to disappointments,
that they may learn to accept themselves
and not lose heart.

We pray for all young people,
that they may be generous and honest
toward their parents,
that they do not write off or hate
the older generation,
but respect the past,
and, above all, that they should be
faithful to their friends
and unselfish in love,
that they may not indulge
in what is cheap and futile,
that they may not ruin the lives of others,
but be ready to make this world
a better place to live in.
We ask these things for them
of the Lord our God.

Let us pray
for those who are in the prime of life,
that their lives may be fruitful,
that they may not be self-seeking,
but seek the welfare of others.
We pray for all adults,
whether married or single,
that they may not be lonely,
complacent or closed to others,
but that they may go on
seeking each others' friendship
and thus grow in humanity.
Let us pray also
for those who cannot find satisfaction
and those who have failed
in work or in life,
that they may place their hopes
in the future
and not lose faith in God our father
who does not want us to be lost.

Let us pray
for all old people,
that they may stay young in heart,
that they may have wisdom and openness
and not be conservative or envious,
but that they may allow latitude to young people.
Let us pray for the aged,
that they may not be left behind in life,
but still put their experience
to good use in the service of others

and be treated with respect and affection.
We also pray
for those who are troubled with illness
and for all who are anxious
and afraid of death.
We pray that they may be given light and faith,
a spirit of surrender and peace.

Let us pray for ourselves,
that, young or old,
we may constantly be made
new men by God's grace,
that we may banish from our midst
all discord and mistrust,
that we do not break with each other,
even though we may be separated by age
and that God may keep us together
as father and son,
as mother and daughter,
as one family
and one people.

Lord our God,
we place these things before you
as well as so many other requests
and prayers that occur to us.
You will hear us, knowing
that we wish to pray only
for your kingdom
and for peace and truth,
and that we pray

that your will be done
at all times in us
and from day to day.
We ask you this
through Jesus Christ. Amen.

+ *Mary's song of thanksgiving*

I sing with all my soul and praise the Lord,
my heart is glad because of God my savior,
for he has looked upon his humble servant
and who am I to merit his attention?

I may henceforth regard myself as happy
because my God has done great things for me,
and every generation gives assent—
the Lord is mighty and his name is holy.

He gives his grace anew in every age
to all who live in reverence with him.
Grace is his strength, but he unmasks all pride
and strips us bare of our self-conceit.

He dethrones those who hold authority
and poor and humble people he makes great.
He gives in great abundance to the hungry
and sends the rich away with empty hands.

His servant Israel he has remembered,
he has been merciful to all his people,
for so had been his promise to our fathers,
to Abraham and to his sons for ever.

THE SON OF MEN

And he was transfigured before them.

Mark 9, 2

+ God, this word we call you by
is almost dead and meaningless,
transient and empty
like all the words men use.
We ask you
to renew its force and meaning,
to make it once again
a name that brings your promise to us.
Make it a living word
which tells us
that you will be for us
as you have always been—
trustworthy and hidden
and very close to us,
our God, now and for ever.

+ Lord God,
we speak with reverence
and in hope of blessing
the name of Jesus, your son.
In the days of his mortal life,
he bore our frailties
but in his anxiety he prayed to you
and you heard him.
Help us in our weakness
so that we too
may always cling to you
whatever happens to us,
to you, the God of our life.

+ You have given your son to us.
He was a man and, like us, mortal.
He can understand and help us
because he too has suffered
and was put to the test.
We pray that we too
may mature in adversity
and be able to help
and understand each other
and that we may,
in all temptation and sinfulness,
always hold onto him,
our Lord and God,
today and all the days
of our lives.

+ Eternal God,
you have invested
your own name and power
in a man, Jesus of Nazareth,
our brother.
But he lived without power
in this world.
You gave him the right to speak—
he is your word—
but he could not find a hearing.
We ask you
that we may recognize
in him, this man of sorrows,
our only savior,
God-with-us,
all the days of our lives.

+ Lord God, like Abraham
who was called by you,
we try to believe
that you give life
to the dead
and call into being
the things that do not exist.
And we believe that you
raised your son Jesus from the dead
to deliver us.
We worship you
because that is your love
for the world, and we entreat you
that neither future, nor sin
nor death
may ever separate us
from your love in Jesus,
the son of men,
who lives with you
now and for ever.

+ Lord God,
you sent your son into the world
with no other certainty
but that he had to suffer and to die.
He fulfilled his mission to the end.
And in this way he became
a source of life and joy.
We ask you
to perfect our joy
and let the world see
that he is living
here among us
everywhere on earth.

+ Lord God,
as a miracle of humanity and love,
as a word that makes men free,
your son has come to us,
and where he comes
life is no longer dark and fearful.
We pray that he
may come to life among us here,
that we may not be ensnared in confusion,
obsessed with doubt and discord,
but that we may be filled
with faith and courage,
simplicity and peace.

+ *The song of the son of man*

Of all the many people
God chose one single nation
to cross the pathless desert,
go under heavy clouds,
be exiled and abandoned
and hear the word of God,
to understand the message
and, having ears to hear with,
to hear and understand.

A remnant of this nation
was faithful to the message
and did not lose the friendship
of their creator God.
Of all the many women
there was but one alone
found worthy to conceive him,
the word of God, man's brother,
God's own beloved son.

The son of man's vocation
and task was to accomplish
the will of God and serve us
by suffering and death.
The son of God, in dying
a slave's death on the cross,
became for us and all men
the soul of our existence,
the savior of the world.

+ Lord God,
you know what is the matter with men
that we shall never be able
to take sin away from the world,
but that we make each other hard and bitter
and take one another's lives.
We implore you, God, for grace,
for the sake of Jesus Christ, your son,
who bore the sins of the world
with him into death.
He lives with you
in the fellowship of the Holy Spirit
today and every day
for ever and ever.

+ Eternal God,
we bear your name, your imprint.
You have impressed your son,
your likeness on us
and we are yours.
We ask you
that we may be like him to a man,
that we may mirror your existence
and reflect your grace
in all our human contacts,
as Christ our brother did
in serving this world
once and for all time.

+ O God,
you have taken our desire
for enduring life so seriously
that you swore to love us
and be faithful to us always.
We hold you to that promise
and ask you
to make our lowly bodies
like the body of Jesus your son,
to make us happy for ever
with him
who lives for you and for this world
today and every day
for ever and ever.

+ We have your promise, God,
to live by and your word
to hold onto.
We rely on your providence
in all that may befall us—
you know what is good for us.
And in hope and fear
and confidence in you
we face the future.
Living or dead, we ask you
that we may be yours,
named after you
and secure with you
together with Jesus Christ our brother,
your son for ever.

+ Almighty God,
you awoke in your son,
Jesus of Nazareth,
the desire to be
man without power or prestige
in this world.
And he experienced in his person
what that meant,
dying, as he did,
like a slave on the cross.
Let us, we beseech you,
recognize in him your power and wisdom
and give us faith
in your power to bring
even the dead to life again,
faith in you, the living God,
today and every day
for ever and ever.

+ You, God, are not
as we think you are.
You have shown us
that you are different
in Jesus Christ, your son,
light of your light,
who humbly trod the path
that anyone treads in this world—
this is how you have saved us.
We thank you
for coming to us
and for being so close to us
in this man, Jesus,
today and every day.

Let us pray
that Christ's own attitude of mind may grow in us,
that we may be tolerant toward each other
and respect our fellow men,
that we may be easily hurt rather than unfeeling
and powerless and without prestige
rather than unapproachable and proud.
Let us pray
for mildness and humility
in our dealings with all people,
that we may be faithful to those
who are unfaithful to us,
for patience and a forgiving spirit.

Let us pray
for all those who have dedicated themselves
to the service of their neighbors,
for those who are engaged in social work,
for all members of charitable organizations,
for all who nurse the sick and the aged.
Let us pray
that they do not do their work of love
only to be seen by men
and that they resist the temptation
to exert power over their fellows
but that, in all simplicity,
they give themselves to others as Jesus did.

Let us pray
for all those in power,
for those who rule the world
that they may not endanger peace;
for those responsible for our welfare
that they may care for the poor and needy;
and for those who are engaged in education and research,
that they may serve the truth
and increase our opportunities for a happy life.

Let us pray
for all ministers and priests
and for all who hold some office in their church,
that they may imitate the High Priest Jesus
who did not think his dignity a thing to be grasped.
And let us pray for all churches
that they may continue,
in poverty and without pretensions,
the work of service to all men
that Jesus came to do.
We pray that they may avoid compulsion
and offer no false security,
but present the gospel to all men
and inspire faith.

Together with those
who have gone before us in faith,
with Mary, the mother of our Lord,
and with all the saints,
with our bishop
and with our Pope,

we pray
for peace in the world
and for the unity of the whole church of God,
so that the world may believe and see
that he is undivided love,
our God, now and for ever.

+ God,
you did not display yourself
in power and majesty,
but, in the face of our expectations
and failure to understand,
you showed yourself
in the weakness and folly
of Jesus your son.
We ask you
that we may understand
your first and last word
in this man on earth,
your strength, your wisdom
and the meaning of our lives.

+ Lord God,
you are not far above us
and beyond our reach.
The place you seek in this world
is neither prominent
nor exalted.
You went the way of all seed.
You are as ordinary
and as inconspicuous as bread
and, like bread,
so necessary to life.
We hope
that we may see you
in all seed,
in all bread,
in all your people.
And so
give us new eyes to see with
and new strength to believe,
today and all the days
of our lives.

Before the paschal feast, when Jesus' hour
had come at last to leave this world,
he showed his love for us, his own—
the son of God the father, like a slave,
washed his disciples' feet.

Then at the supper with his friends, the twelve,
he broke the bread and took the cup
and gave his life in bread and wine
as tokens of his everlasting love,
body and blood of Christ.

I am the way, the truth, the life, he said,
I am the vine—abide in me.
I am who am, forgiving sins,
my peace I leave with you, he told his friends,
not as the world gives peace.

When Jesus' hour had come to leave his friends,
he raised his eyes to heaven and prayed
for those he left behind on earth
that they might all be one so that the world
might come to believe in God.

Then, going to the garden, Jesus prayed,
remove this cup from me, but let
me do your will and not my own.
A friend betrayed him there, one of the twelve,
sold him to die for us.

+ You are not here, God.
You have passed by
invisible as the wind
and inaudible as the calm.
You have always relied
on our reverence and
our faith in you.
If your dealings with us
are so superhuman,
you must be patient
and forgive us
if we have no other answer
but your own ineffable name,
so strange and so familiar to us,
the name we pronounce for ever.

+ *Prayers of petition for Good Friday*

Let us pray
for this world, which is sighing
and groaning for redemption,
for the whole of suffering mankind in the present age,
for all those who are the victims of war and racial conflict,
for those who are overwhelmed by natural disasters,
for all who meet with any kind of accident,
for those who are in any kind of danger,
let us pray:

Lord God
you want the well-being of men
and not their destruction.
Take all violence from our midst.
Extinguish hatred in our hearts.
Curb the passion in us
that makes us seek each others' lives.
Give peace on earth
to all mankind.
We ask you this
through Jesus Christ, our Lord.

Let us pray
for those who are deprived and live in poverty,
for all who are despairing
and feel themselves to be beyond help,
for all whose minds are disturbed or who are mentally ill,
for those who suffer physically for years
and whose bodies are gradually broken down.
Let us pray
for all who must die alone
without the hope of life after death
and without faith in the resurrection of their bodies.

Lord God,
you have made us mortal
and we must die.
Do not, we beseech you,
take our lives away for ever,
you who are
a God of the living.
We ask you this
for Jesus' sake,
today and every day
for ever and ever.

Let us pray
for all those who are in great difficulty—
for those who have lost their faith
in man and love, their faith in God,
for those who seek truth but cannot find it.
Let us pray for all married people
who have drifted apart from each other
and for all priests who have broken down
under the strain of their office.

Lord God,
you are the comfort of the sorrowful
and the strength of the tortured.
Hear the prayers
of all men in distress
and all who appeal to your mercy,
so that they may recognize with joy
that you have helped them
in every ordeal,
through Jesus Christ, our Lord.

Let us pray
for the town we live and work in,
for all the people in it who are lonely,
for those whose voices are never heard
and those who find no friends.
Let us pray
for the homeless and those without shelter
and for all who are disheartened
and feel that they have been betrayed.

Lord God,
you have given us
a place to live in,
a town and space to build in
and people to live with.
Open our eyes to each other.
Make us humble enough
to help other people
and comfort them,
so that a little of your love
may be seen in this town,
through Jesus Christ, our Lord.

Let us ask the Lord our God for forgiveness
for the suffering that we cause to others,
for our forgetfulness and neglect of others,
for our lack of understanding for each other,
for speaking ill of other people
and for the bitterness and spite
we so often feel toward our fellows,
for not being able to forgive.
Let us pray for forgiveness
of all the sins that men, in their helplessness,
commit against each other.

Lord God,
we behold you
in the broken body
of Jesus our brother
and know who you are
for this world.
In the broken bread
we receive the promise
that you are the forgiveness
of our sins.
We pray, for the sake of him
in whom everything is consummated,
let us enter into your peace,
whoever we are,
and send your Spirit upon us
so that we may be
open and receptive
to you and pray to you
with the words of the prayer
that he taught us—

Our father, who art in heaven,
hallowed be thy name.
Thy kingdom come.
Thy will be done,
on earth, as it is in heaven.
Give us this day our daily bread,
and forgive us our trespasses,
as we forgive those who trespass against us,
and lead us not into temptation,
but deliver us from evil.
For thine is the kingdom
and the power and the glory,
for ever and ever. Amen.

Your word comes to those
who are severely tried and tested
and who believe, yet doubt
and are afraid.
We speak your name
when we are powerless
and at the end of our knowledge
we still hand on your name
we give you away
with empty hands.
So we become,
forsaken by you and crucified,
your power, your wisdom,
your beloved son.

DEATH AND LIFE

There is hope for a tree
if it be cut down
that it will sprout again
and that its shoots will not cease.

But a man dies
and is laid low;
a man breathes his last
and where is he?

As a river
wastes away and is dried up,
so a man lies down
and rises not again.

Job 14, 7-12

+ Lord God, you were happy to give us
the light of our eyes
and to let us be born.
You did not make us
for darkness and death,
but so that we should, with all our hearts,
live and come closer to you.
Be merciful to us then
and take us by the hand
and lead us to life
today and for ever.

+ O God, give your glory
and your promised future
to this dead person.
We cannot believe
that his life has been spent in vain
and that all he meant to other people
is lost now he is no longer with us.
But we share the faith
by which he held onto you
to the very end
to you, his God and ours,
to you living for us
today and every day
for ever and ever.

We thank you, God,
for this man who was so near and dear to us
and who has now been taken from us.
We thank you
for the friendship that went out from him
and the peace he brought.
We thank you
that through suffering he learned obedience
and that he became a person others could love
while he was with us here on earth.

We pray
that nothing of this man's life
will be lost,
but that it will be
of benefit to the world;
that all that he held sacred
may be respected
by those who follow him
and that everything in which he was great
may continue to mean much to us
now that he is dead.
We ask you
that he may go on living
in his children,
in their hearts and minds,
their courage and their conscience.

We ask you
that we who were associated with him
may now, because of his death,
be even more closely associated with each other
and that we may, in this togetherness
and peace and friendship here on earth,
always be deeply conscious of your promise
to be faithful to us in death.

+ *For ourselves, who are still living*

Let us pray for ourselves,
who are severely tested by this death,
that we do not try to minimize this loss
or seek refuge from it in words
and also that we do not brood over it
so that it overwhelms us
and isolates us from others.
May God grant us new courage
and confidence to face life.

Let us pray
for those who go on blindly,
unable to overcome their sorrow,
that they may be saved from their despair
for God's sake and for the sake of their dead
that God may be a fellow man for them
who can, in his silence, comfort them
and bear their burden with them.

Let us pray
for those who have to go on living alone
after the death of their partner,
for those who mourn
the death of a child,
a friend or close relative
and all who have suffered
an unspeakable loss.

Let us pray
for those whom illness
has cut off from their fellows
and who cannot work
or are denied all freedom of movement
and are alone with themselves.
Let us pray too
for all who are in constant conflict
with others and who cannot
find an answer to this problem
and for those who cannot speak their minds
and must be silent and stand alone.

Let us pray
for all who are discouraged
by the hardness of men,
that they may not hate the light of life
and become embittered,
and think that evil is stronger than good,
but that they may keep an open heart
in hope and expectation.

Let us pray
for all who die and are not mourned,
but are ignored in death
like a stone by the wayside.
Let us pray
for all who are lost in war and prison,
for those who have committed suicide
and those who are lonely in life and death,
that God may hear them
and keep them in his heart.

+ God, we keep watch
beside this dead person
and pray for him.
His body is cold now
and he is dead,
but we want to keep
his name alive among us.
Yet we know
that even this is impossible.
He will die in us too,
his name will fade
in our memory
and even the sorrow
that we feel now
will be taken away from us.
We shall go on living
without him.
We ask you, then,
that he, living with you,
may watch over us
and intercede for us,
that he may remind you
unceasingly of our names
as Jesus does,
a man near you
in your eternity.

Brothers and sisters,
we are gathered together here
around this dead body,
all that is left to us of this man,
to pay our last respects to him
and to do justice to his life and death.
Keeping our eyes fixed
on the cross of Jesus Christ
we say in groping faith
that this is not the end,
that our God is a God of the living.

Rather than his body
we are left with the name of this man, . . .
which we speak now with reverence and affection
and pray
Lord God, remember this name
which he was given by other people
and by which he is known
even though he is dead,
the name that you have written
on the palm of your hand.
As a sign of our hope
that God will give a new and immortal body
to this man and to all of us
and to bear witness
to our faith in the resurrection,
I bless this dead body
in the name of the Father and of the Son

and of the Holy Spirit.

The body is blessed
with water

Let us now go in peace
and take him, whom we have had among us
during this past hour
for the last time, to his grave.
We let him go
out of our keeping
and place him
in the earth, in the care of the living God,
in the name of the Father and of the Son
and of the Holy Spirit.

Flowers are placed
on the coffin

May our prayers accompany him.

The coffin is taken out.
This song is sung:

No one lives for himself,
no one dies for himself.
We live and we die
for God our Lord
and we are the Lord's.

+ A song of life and death

God calls a man to life,
we know not how or why,
he has to give himself
and live only to die.

We know not when it was
that God at first began,
because of his great love,
his history with man.

We do know that he chose
from all mankind one nation
and sent his word to them
to bring them to salvation.

He led this captive race
from Egypt through the sea
and following his word
they were at last made free.

And yet, to bring fulfillment
to what he had begun,
God sent among his people
the God-man, his own son.

And now as God's new people
we are redeemed by him
who died a bitter death
to save the world from sin.

We too, like him, must suffer—
he was God's word made man—
we too must lose our life
to carry out God's plan.

Christ gave his life for us,
his body is our bread,
and we who share his life
will rise up from the dead.

+ You did not make us as angels, God,
but as men, to live on earth,
full of love and hatred,
experiencing ecstasy and misery
and boring and delighting ourselves and others.
This is how we are to live all our lives.
Will you therefore say to us
what you have never said to an angel,
"You are my son.
I have brought you forth today
and I will be your father"?
Say this, Lord God, to this man now
and tell him,
"Here is your place,
with Jesus Christ, at my right hand,
son of man for ever."

We pray to you
for all who are crucified
like your son,
for all who are forsaken by you.
For all who cannot endure their fate,
for all who suffer
and cannot see why.

For all who are rebellious
or exhausted and stunned,
for those who are bitter and cynical,
turned in on themselves
and scornful of others—
make them mild and open their eyes again
to the goodness that is possible among men
and to your creation and your future.

For all who are viewed with mistrust,
who live under the pressure
of suspicion and evil gossip,
for all whose self-confidence has been undermined
by the harsh criticism of others,
for all who are misunderstood
and who never hear a kind word
or meet anyone who will accept them.

For all who are anxious or inhibited,
for those whose consciences are warped and not free,
for all who are tense and restless,
uncertain or at their wits' end.
For all who are the victims
of blackmail or corruption,
for all those whose lives are wrecked
by their involvement with the gods
and powers of darkness—
that they may, in their defenselessness,
resemble your son Jesus
who was defenseless
in the hands of men.

For all who have to live with injustice,
who are caught up in an inhuman system
and who cannot make any headway under it.
For all soldiers at the front
who have to fight and kill
against their will and against their consciences.

For all those who want war
and whose aim is to divide men.
For those who make money
from the destruction of others.
For all whose minds are poisoned and dangerous—
that they may be freed from their inhumanity
and granted forgiveness.

For all who have lost heart
because of so much evil in the world.
But also for those who are optimistic,
for those who radiate strength
and can offer friendship—
that they may not fail when they are tested
and that we may never lack their companionship.

We pray to you
for all who have no form or beauty
to look up to,
for those who cannot keep up with others,
for children who have been born unlucky,
for all who are disturbed or handicapped,
for those who are incurably ill.
We ask you
that we may discover the meaning
of their presence in this world.

A MAN OF PEACE

They did, however, question
what this rising from the dead meant.

Mark 9, 10

+ You have done the impossible, God,
for all who are born.
What no eye has seen,
nor ear heard,
nor the heart of man conceived,
you have prepared, God,
for those who seek you—
Jesus, the son of men,
resurrected from the dead.
We thank you for creating us
so that we might have
such grace bestowed upon us
and for being as you are,
a God of the living.

+ We worship and admire you, God,
because you have shown your power
in Jesus Christ,
raising him from the dead
and setting him at your right hand,
exalting him above all powers
and giving him a name
which is above every name in this world.
We ask you
that we who believe in him
may be of his mind as well,
that we may be a sign
of his life,
light and peace to all
who seek you, today
and every day of our lives.

+ *A hymn for Easter night*

For you who are present here tonight,
for you who know of death and darkness
I sing this hymn that rises like a light
and like a tree of life.
I sing to you of Jesus Christ.
He is the song on every tongue,
he is the word passed down to us
from the beginning and through all time
up to this night, the word
that we shall go on speaking all our lives
so that God's faithfulness is known
among our children and that his covenant
with us may never die.

O holy, most high God,
we praise you, lowly as we are,
with the voices you have given us
and in the name of this world, all your people,
that multitude which none can count,
we venerate your glory and your power
and throw ourselves upon your mercy.

For everything passes, but you remain.
Your name, your grace continue
despite all our sins, for you are God.
You do not tire of this your world.
You set so much store by human happiness
that you gave everything to be our God.

You showed yourself to us in Jesus Christ,
enlightened our darkness in your son.
In him we behold you, God the father,
in him we receive your future and your trust.

He is your word, the light of the world,
He is the new Adam, the son of man,
born of the earth and spoken by you
to the world before all time.
He is that word made flesh among us.
His life among us was like other men's
and he was broken at the hands of men
and so he met his death.

Then you did what transcends our understanding—
on this night he was resurrected from the dead,
on this night he disarmed and conquered death.
He who was foolish and had no power
to save himself became your power and wisdom.
Your foolishness, God, is wiser than men
and your weakness is stronger than men.
How inscrutable are your ways, O God,
and how unfathomable is your love!
Who was your counsellor, God,
that you thus gave yourself to the world?

Everything that exists is yours.
We owe all that we are to you.
All things and all these words are for you
and we trust in you, our God.
Would you ever let us down?

+ Who are we, God,
that you have done
to one of us
such great things?
You gave Jesus Christ,
the son of men,
eternal life.
And in your eyes
that gift was not enough
and you gave all men grace
in hope and fear
and gave it abundantly.
We venture, then, to ask you this—
fulfill what you have begun
and make us fruitful
all the days of our lives,
as wide as the world,
as high as heaven,
with Jesus your son
now and for ever.

+ *Of this earth*

We are as you have made us—
we belong heart and soul to this earth.
Keep us in this grace,
make us faithful to your creation
and teach us to recognize,
in gratitude and delight,
that everything that you have done
is good.

+ God,
you stand up for us
like a father for his son
or a man for his friend.
And you do more than this,
so deeply do you care for us
and no man can prevent you
from being our God.
We rely on you,
we wait for you
and we trust in your name.
You are too great a truth
to be expressed in our words.
You are our space and time
now and for ever.

+ God,
we have not seen your son
with our own eyes,
nor have we touched his body
with our hands,
but we still try
to believe in him.
We ask you
to give us your power
and send us your Holy Spirit
who will guide us
into all the truth
in this life
and always.

+ God, it is your happiness and life
that one son of man,
of all the men born into this world,
should go on living with us
and that one name should inspire us
from generation to generation—Jesus Christ.
We are gathered here
in your presence
to pray that we may
hear and see him
and pass on his name
to all who wish to receive it.
Let your Spirit move us
to receive him from each other
and from you, this man
who is our future,
who lives with you
for all men and for the whole world.

+ Eternal God,
you have given your own name
to Jesus, our brother.
He is the Lord,
your first-born son.
We pray to you
that we may bear your name,
if need be, like a burden
on our shoulders
or like a fire in our mouths—
your Holy Spirit
who makes us sons
and prays in us
and calls to you
today and every day.

+ *To our Lord Jesus Christ*

You are the voice of the living God,
light and likeness of his glory.
You did not spare your own life,
but shed your blood and gave your soul—
you went out to seek us
and you died to find us.
We pray that,
strengthened and inspired by you,
we may do for each other
what you have done for us.
Give us the strength to be
as good to each other as God.

You are a man like us,
blood of our blood
and, bearing the name of God,
you are exalted in his light,
the son of God.
But do not be remote from us,
hidden and unapproachable!
Pray for us with your human voice
and send us your Spirit
that we may come to life
and make this world
a fit place to live in
and meet him, your father and ours,
now and in the life to come.

Let us pray
for all our fellow men,
for everyone with whom we are associated,
for all those entrusted to our care,
for the families we have been given,
for our friends and those we love,
for all those with whom we have daily contact
and whom we represent before God in prayer.

Let us pray
for a vital and humane society,
for mutual trust and solidarity
wherever men work together
in industry and business
and for honesty in all transactions,
for good conditions of employment
and fair wage contracts.
Let us pray that our country's future
may be planned with expert care
and that the same care may be devoted
to the just and equal distribution of our prosperity.

Let us pray
for the increase of respect and discreet love
in our hospitals and mental hospitals,
our rehabilitation centers and old people's homes
and that we may always have a place
for people who are different from ourselves.
Let us pray
for all who are unhappy and unattractive,

that they may not be cast out or neglected,
and for those who are difficult to live with,
that they may meet with patience and understanding.

Let us pray
for those in high positions in the world
and for all who are called to leadership,
that they may make other men's lives secure
and that they do not yield
to the power of corruption and injustice,
but champion the cause of the poor
and the underprivileged.
Let us also pray
for all who are engaged in international politics,
that they may never cease in their attempts to find peace
and that there may be an end
to the senseless destruction of so many human lives.

Let us pray
for all those, throughout the world,
who believe in the gospel,
that they may grow in grace and humanity.
Let us also pray for all churches,
that they may not lay up treasures on earth
or become monuments to a past age,
clinging to what is already dead
and remote from people of today,
but that they may be converted
and receive the spirit of Jesus, our Lord,
who is the light and life, hope and peace
of this world, for ever and ever.

He was a man like us,
a man who died.
He is a name.
They say he is alive
and there are those who say
he lives for them
and that he makes them free
to share in joy and sorrow
and that he keeps them going.
He is the way, the truth,
the life, they say, their future.
He is a word
as long as there are men
in this world of hard facts
remote yet near
in every word he is
a man of peace
who suffers death.
And if there is a God,
if you, God, can exist,
then you are he
and he, for me, is you.
Then I will stay near him.
That is enough.

And Jesus perceived in himself
that power had gone forth from him.

Mark 5, 30

+ This is the day, Lord,
when you give the breath of life
to this world,
when you enkindle
a fire of love in men.
Today is the day
that we are called together
to be your Church.
We thank you with the words,
the seed that you have sown in us
and we admire you
in the power of the Holy Spirit
and joyfully proclaim you
as our father.

+ You have kindled
your light in us
and you have inspired us
with your Holy Spirit.
We pray that we,
impelled by this Spirit,
may always seek the truth
and revere your word
and that we may find Jesus,
your son, your life,
your servant and our way.

✝ You are our origin and father—
ours, mine and every man's
in this world.
As long as there are men on earth
you can be found—
we meet you unexpectedly
wherever we may go.
We ask you, then,
to make us new once more, original,
so that we may begin each day anew
with our fellow men
and so find you, God,
today and all the days of our lives.

✝ Lord God,
your kingdom is here
hidden and close to us—
someone to care for
and people to live for.
Your will is done on earth
everywhere
wherever men live and die
for each other.
We pray therefore
that we may gradually
accomplish this from day to day
and thus come to know
your name, and find you,
our father for ever.

+ *In the Holy Spirit*

We worship you, Holy Spirit of God,
and we may only guess, as best we can,
who you are for us.
We call you by human names and words
so that we need not be entirely silent.
We open up our hearts to receive you
that we may learn
how deeply and invisibly you are present everywhere.
You are the air we breathe,
the distance we gaze into,
the space that surrounds us.
You are the kindly light
in which men are attractive to each other.
You are the finger of God
with which he playfully ordered the universe.
You are the sensitive love
with which he created us.
We pray to you, Spirit of God, creator,
complete the work you have begun,
prevent the evil we are capable of doing
and inspire us toward what is good—
to faithfulness and patience,
to compassion and gentleness,
and waken in us friendship
for every living being
and with joy for everything
that is good and human.

Everything that lives grows only by your power.
Your activity is strange and beyond all human words.
You are hidden deep inside us
like yeast, a seed of fire.
You are our will to live,
the love that keeps us here on earth
and ties us to our God.
You urge us on to go on to the end
and to endure everything,
not to give way and to go on hoping,
as love does.
You are the soul of all our prayers
so there is nothing we may not expect from you—
wisdom to understand each other,
readiness to help each other
and everything we need.
If you are God's gift to us.
Be present here among us, then,
God in us.

You speak in silence
and all languages interpret you.
You are the truth of all words,
their permanence and their comfort
and every man who listens with an open mind
can hear you in his own language
and in his own life.
Put words into our mouths, then,
that comfort and shed light,
make us alive to justice and to right,
groan in us for a new creation,
guide our hearts and our faith,
let our thoughts and our labors be fruitful
and give us the bread of peace.

You are the breath and the fire
with which the word of God is spoken,
the wind on which the gospel is borne
anywhere and to anyone in the world.
It is your work and the wonder of your inspiration
whenever men experience that Jesus lives.
That we follow him, that he becomes our way,
that men acknowledge that he is
worth all the trouble that this life can bring—
this is your enthusiasm and your power in us.
We ask you to perpetuate this
so that we may go on believing
and persevere with him we have not seen
and go on groping for him who is our God and brother.
We ask you this
for all our weakness and the brevity of our lives on earth.
You are the life-giving Spirit who frees us,
dangerous and compelling
for those who cling to worldly goods and ties of blood.
You are both promise and uncertainty,
both poverty and grace.
No one is innocent if you are not with him,
but those who receive you—their sins are forgiven.
So you were poured out over this world,
so you are sent even now to the Church
which, orphaned and formless,
waits for a new beginning from you.

We pray to you—give us life,
as you breathed life and grace
into the soul of man in the beginning
and as you raised Jesus, our brother,
to life from the dead.
Give life and meaning
to the mortal body of his Church.
Remind us of everything
that he lived for.
Make us fire of your fire,
light of your light,
as the son of men, Jesus,
is light of the eternal light in you
and God of God,
today and every day,
for ever and ever.
Amen.

+ *Hardly at all*

Walking backwards
I come to you
my eyes open
my feet wrong
in my bitterness
I come to you
cradle of my father
town like an earthen
vessel, you, stubborn
vaults of water
nails of flowers
rain dull light.

+ *Man and woman,*
husband and wife,
person and person

But we are people, ways of the past,
and we must live close to the ground,
with imperfect love we walk around
and whether up or down we fall at last.

Hans Andreus

1

God, it is your work and your promise if love is found
in this world and if there is any intercourse among
men. We pray that, as man and wife, as friends and
neighbors, we may follow the example of your son,
Jesus Christ, his example of love and respect for his
fellow men, so that we may, in his spirit, be happy and
believe that you are the source of all love, that you
are love itself, our God and our father.

2

You who created people as man and woman you know
that it is not good for us to be alone. Renew therefore
your covenant between person and person and create
a bond of affection between heart and heart. Be as close
to us as the body of the other and let us experience
that everything that you have made is good.

3

All of us owe our happiness to you. You have created
us to live for other people and to find peace. So we pray
for those who do not find their happiness and peace
as man and wife, but who look for friendship with
others who are more meaningful and real to them. We
pray for all these people whom we so often avoid.
We pray that they may be able to put their affections
to good use, that they may learn to live with their
inclinations and the difficult burden they have to bear
and that they may become full human beings, not
despised and shunned, but fully accepted, as a sign that
you, God, will accept us all just as we are, for Jesus
Christ's sake.

4

God, you are intimately bound to all of us by your
faithful covenant with man. We ask you to let us
experience your faithfulness in good times and in bad.
We also pray that we may, in your name, find the
strength to love and honor those who are given to us,
to help them and remain faithful to them all our lives
until death, for your eternity.

When God created man
he saw it was not good
for him to be alone
and therefore that he should
give him a fitting help.
He made you man and wife
in form just like himself
to share this earthly life.

No man who is not loved
most deeply by a mate
can find a true response,
and so the married state,
this union of a pair,
was made for you to find
response in sharing life
in one flesh and one mind.

You two will lead one life
in poverty or wealth,
in sorrow and in joy,
in sickness or in health
and God will be with you
whatever is your fate—
he is your bread and wine.
This mystery is great.

If we could not hear and understand,
if we could not speak, God,
we should be nowhere—
unable to approach each other
and strangers to ourselves.
But you have made people of us—
we have been born and are no longer speechless
and you have attuned us to each other
as man and woman,
as mouth and mouth,
as word and answer,
as question and counter-question.

We thank you for the language of men,
that great heart, that deep memory
in which so much wisdom
is hidden and preserved,
for the precious words and living names
which have been handed down to us.
They hold us tight and yet surprise us.
They are older and greater than we are.
We thank you
that we are so much part of your history
that we are called by names
and are not lost to our children.

We thank you for today,
for the present age in which we live,
a secular city of words and facts
and of people involved with each other.
We pray
for safety in all these human contacts,
for people who do good
and who are mild and merciful.
We pray
that our words may not spread darkness in the world,
that they may not be harmful
or outlaw anyone,
that we may not chase after lies
or cause a confusion of tongues,
but sow joy and reap recognition,
your new covenant, Lord, with this world.

We pray
for those who unlock the future with their words
and disclose new truth,
for poets and philosophers
who show us new paths
and praise man's life in verse,
that they may reverence and reveal
all that is human
and help to relieve the tension in our lives
and increase happiness.
We pray for all
whose task is to administer justice,
that they may go beneath the surface of hard facts
and discover more truth,
and especially that they may leave room for forgiveness
and a new beginning.

We thank you, God,
for having spoken your name
in our language and in our present age
and for living in this world, a human word
that is as vulnerable as any word can be.
Extend your presence
into the universe of our thoughts and dreams
and to the work of our hands.
Inspire our language
and give it meaning and power of expression.
Let us receive your Spirit
into our life and dialogue with other men.
Let us recognize in all mankind,
in every man and woman of flesh and words,
your son, our Lord,
your word made flesh, your glory
now and for ever.

+ I pray to you, my God,
and call you by your name,
but cannot lay hold of you
because you are greater than a name
and smaller than a word,
more silent than all silence in the world.
Make me receptive to you,
give me a living heart
and new eyes
to see you, hidden and invisible,
to take you as you are
when you come without power,
and, in my weakness, in my death,
to know who you are.

We thank you,
Lord God almighty,
for you are a God of men,
for you are not ashamed
to be called our God,
for you know us all by name
for you hold the world in your hands.
And that is why you have created us
and for this purpose called us into life
that we should be all made one with you
to be your people here on earth.
Blessed are you,
creator of all that is,
blessed are you
for giving us a place of freedom and of life,
blessed are you
for the light of our eyes
and for the air we breathe.

We thank you for the whole of creation,
for all the works of your hands,
for all that you have done among us
through Jesus Christ, our Lord.
Therefore, together with all the living
and all who have gone before us in faith,
we praise your name,
O Lord our God,
bowing before you
adoring you, saying:

Holy, holy, holy
Lord of all powers.
Heaven and earth
are full of your glory.
Come and deliver us,
Lord most high.
Blessed is he who comes
in the name of the Lord.
Come and deliver us,
Lord most high.

We thank you, holy father,
Lord our God,
for the sake of Jesus Christ,
your beloved son,
whom you called and sent
to serve us and give us light,
to bring your kingdom
to the poor,
to bring redemption
to all captive people
and to be for ever
and for all mankind
the likeness and the form
of your constant love and goodness.

We thank you
for this unforgettable man
who has fulfilled everything
that is human—
our life and death.
We thank you
because he gave himself,
heart and soul, to this world.

For, on the night that he was delivered up,
he took bread into his hands
and raising his eyes to you,
God, his almighty father,
he gave thanks
and broke the bread
and gave it to his friends
with the words:
take and eat,
this is my body for you.
Do this in memory of me.

He also took the chalice
and, giving thanks to you, said:
this chalice is the new covenant in my blood
shed for you and for all mankind
so that sins may be forgiven.
Every time you drink this chalice,
you will do it in memory of me.

So whenever we eat of this bread
and drink from this chalice,
we proclaim the death of the Lord
until he comes.

Therefore, Lord our God,
we present this sign of our faith
and therefore we call to mind
the suffering and death of your son,
his resurrection from the dead,
his entry into your glory,
recalling that he
who is exalted at your right hand
will intercede for us
and that he will come
to do justice to the living and the dead
on the day that you have appointed.

We beseech you
send over us your Holy Spirit
and give a new face
to this earth that is dear to us.
May there be peace
wherever people live,
the peace that we cannot make ourselves
and that is more powerful than all violence,
your peace like a bond,
a new covenant between all men,
the power of Jesus Christ
here among us.

Then your name will be made holy,
Lord our God,
through him and with him and in him
everywhere on earth
and in this fellowship of the Holy Spirit
this hour and every day
world without end.
Amen.

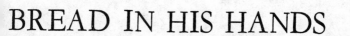

BREAD IN HIS HANDS

Do you not yet
perceive and understand?
Are your hearts hardened?
Having eyes do you not see,
and having ears do you not hear?
And do you not remember,
when I broke five loaves
for the five thousand,
how many baskets full of broken pieces
did you take up?
They said to him, twelve.
And the seven for the four thousand,
how many baskets full of broken pieces
did you take up?
And they said to him, seven.
And he said to them,
Do you not yet understand?

Mark 8, 17-21

+ God, we witness
unheard of things.
You, God, have given power
to Jesus of Nazareth,
whom we recognize as one of us,
to be merciful to others
and to forgive them.
We ask you, God,
for this power, this freedom
to be a healing grace
to all those who live with us
in this world,
as a sign that you are
the forgiveness of all sins.

+ God,
we break bread for one another
and receive the body
of Jesus Christ, your son.
We ask you
that, strengthened by him,
we may live in love and peace
so that he may be present
wherever we speak words
and we may become his body
in this world, for ever.

Bread from seed sown in earth
bread made by human hands
bread tasting of sorrow
and of men of many lands

bread of war and of peace
unchanging daily bread
strange bread of affection
and the stone bread of the dead

bread, our body our all
earned with such bitter sweat
bread, life with our fellows
whom we easily forget

bread without which we die
matter of such great worth
bread shared with each other
throughout all our life on earth.

Bread of life shared with us—
you give yourself as food
you, man among others
and a God of flesh and blood.

+ Lord our God,
you have sown in us your word,
given us your son—
he, who was broken and died for us,
is bread and life
for the world.
We ask you
to let us find strength to tread his path,
to let us be for each other
as fertile as seed
and as nourishing as bread
and thus lead a happy life.

+ We have heard your word, O God,
and have broken bread
for each other.
May this be a sign for us
that you are very near,
that we are your people,
nourished and loved by you.
Never forsake us
and be the light around us
and our firm ground
and even more,
be our future, our father.

+ Lord God,
we have received your word
and have tasted your truth—
Jesus Christ, the son of your love
delivered into the hands of men
and put to death.
We pray
that we may never be scandalized
by this man,
but take him as he is
and that we may learn to see
that we owe our lives to him
today and for ever.

+ You set off with us, O God,
and have trodden our path.
You can also lead us to our rightful home
and perfect us.
We pray
that Jesus may be our guide
and that we may live
with each other in his light.
And let us grow in the faith
that the future is his
today and every day
for ever and ever.

+ God, should we who ask and seek
be given no reply?
It seems as though you never speak.
Father, know that I believe,
but captured in my doubt
I pray and what shall I receive?

When we ask you, God, for bread
will you give us a stone?
Are you our God or are you dead?

Father, are you never near
to us who plead for grace?
It is as if you do not hear.

Let us pray
for the world that is unmeasurable,
a society of millions of people
and newspapers full of news.
Let us pray
for the smaller world around us,
for the people who belong to us,
for the members of our families,
our friends and those who share our worries
and those who depend on us.

Let us pray
for those with big names,
for the leaders of governments
and those whose words and actions
will influence the situation in the world—
that they may not tolerate injustice,
seek refuge in violence
or make rash and ill-considered decisions
about the future of other people.
Let us also pray for all
who live in the shadow of world events,
for those who are never noticed
but who do their duty and remain obscure,
for all who are automatically just,
ordinary and likeable,
for mothers who look after their families
and for doctors and nurses
who do their work without talking about it.

Let us pray for all our fellow men
whose pain and misery come to us every day
in the newspapers and on the television,
for the victims of racial discrimination
in America and elsewhere,
for the millions who are starving to death,
for the countless victims
of fratricide in Indonesia,
and for the people of Vietnam
who have been suffering for so long.
And let us pray
for everyone in our own district
who is a victim of illness or misfortune,
suspicion or uncertainty,
for those who threaten the lives of others
whether in big or in small ways,
and for ourselves
that we may not become cruel and intolerant
and live at the expense of others.

143

Let us pray
for the Church of God in this world,
for all who know they are called
to live and proclaim the gospel,
for those who are in authority,
for the Vatican in Rome
and the World Council of Churches in Geneva,
for bishops, church-wardens and elders,
ministers and priests,
for those who have become worn out in office,
for all in monastic orders
that they may not become tired
of silence and the name of God,
and for ourselves
that God may make us fit
for the service of love,
his work in this world,
that we may be moved by his Spirit
to tread the path of faith and perseverance
and that we, like Jesus our Lord and guide,
may be a help to all
who fall and cannot carry on.

Let us thank the Lord
for sustaining the world.
We thank him too
for the courage of so many people
and that children are born
and the dead are lamented,
that love exists between men and women
and friendship beyond all frontiers.
We thank him
for the hard work that is done
in factories and universities,
laboratories and studies
and for the energy that is devoted
to spreading free and generous understanding
between so many people.
We pray
that justice and right and loyalty
may be stronger
than injustice and destruction
everywhere in the world, in this town
and in ourselves.

GREATER THAN
OUR HEARTS

*Go home to your friends
and tell them how much
the Lord has done for you.*

Mark 5, 19

＋ Lord God,
we see the sins of the world
in the light of your only son.
Since his coming
to be your mercy toward us
we have come to suspect
how hard and unrelenting
we are toward each other.
We ask you to renew us
according to his example.
Let us grow like him
and no longer repay evil with evil,
but make peace and live in truth
today and every day
of our lives.

＋ God, you are not happy with us
when we make each other unhappy.
You cannot bear it
when we kill and destroy each other.
Break, we pray you,
the cycle of evil
that holds us captive
and let sin die in us
as the sin of the world
died in Jesus your son
and death was killed.
He lives for us
today and every day.

✝ You cannot endure
even one of your people
to be lost, O God.
You seek us
when we stray from you.
You look for us
far more than we seek you.
We cling
to that certainty
and to that promise
and we rely
on your most resourceful love.

✝ We fall, O God,
and can go no farther.
We are paralyzed
and cannot stand again.
Sustained by the faith of your Church
we come to you,
for who can forgive sins
but you alone?
Heal us and raise us up
for the sake of your mercy
and of Jesus, our brother.
Did you not raise him from the dead?
He lives with you
for this world and for all ages.

+ When we were lost, God,
you gave us grace.
When we were strangers and far away
you called us.
Now we have come close to you
accept us whoever we are
and obey the promptings of your heart
in what you do with us.

+ Who should we be, O Lord,
had you not made us?
You saw, received and loved us—
then we sinned against you.
Out of the depths we cry to you,
father,
for your name is printed
indelibly on our minds
and unforgettable
is the memory of your love.
Without any rights
we return to you
and ask you to come to meet us
with open arms
because you are our father
today and every day
of our lives, in all eternity.

⁺ Lord God,
anyone who has finally settled with you
can always go back to you—
there is nothing that cannot be restored with you
only your love will not be revoked.
We pray, God,
remind us of your name
so that we may turn again to you,
be our father
again and again
and give us life
as a happiness we do not deserve
from day to day
until eternity.

⁺ Lord God, we must forgive
those who trespass against us.
These words of yours
cause us embarrassment.
We do the opposite,
insisting on our rights,
unforgiving and lacking grace.
How shall we ever come up to Christ, your son?
Turn us toward him, we pray you,
for he is the living embodiment of grace,
the forgiveness of sins
and greater than all imaginable guilt.
He is perfect justice and righteousness
for this world
and for all ages.

✝ You did not come, O God, to judge us,
but to seek what is lost,
to set free those
who are imprisoned in guilt and fear
and to save us
when our hearts accuse us.
Take us as we are here,
with all that sinful past
of the world.
You are greater than our heart
and greater than all our guilt—
you are the creator
of a new future
and a God of love
for ever and ever.

✝ You do not deny or make light of our sins,
but you forgive us, Lord.
In this way you do justice to us
and show us your truth.
We can go on again,
with the sins of our past,
because you have not condemned us.
We can venture a new beginning
because you accept us as we are.
We thank you
for this opportunity of new life
and ask you
to give us strength not to sin again. **Amen.**

✝ We are indebted to you, Lord God,
for everything, and have always been.
But the reality of your grace
is greater than our debt to you.
We were nowhere
and you called us.
We were servants
and you made us your friends.
Your word became our servant,
your love to the very end.
We do want to owe everything to you
so long as you remain our God,
a God who is so good to this world
that we cannot conceive it
in all eternity.

+ You have forgiven us
for being as we are—
people with hatred and love
in our hearts,
with a rent in our eyes
and words of stone in our mouths.
You came to us
to be human like ourselves,
to become sin.
At your wits' end
and for all eternity
you do not know
what more you can do
than to treat men,
every man,
as more important than yourself.
I am that man.

HERE IN OUR MIDST

Your exile will be long;
build houses
and live in them
and plant gardens
and eat their produce.

Jeremiah 29, 28

+ You have made your dwelling
among us, God,
and you are present
wherever men live—
we cling to this grace.
Make us honor your presence
and make us wise and strong enough
to build each other up
into your city on earth,
the body of Christ,
a world fit to live in,
today and for ever.

+ We ask you for bread and peace
and your answer, God, is
Jesus Christ, your son.
He is bread
for the life of the world,
our hope and our peace.
We pray
that he may be powerful
here in our midst
and that we may find gladness
in this man, whom you have given us
here and now and for ever.

+ Psalm

I will eat of two words only
four can never be enough
distant love, O loving peace.

Not for hunger and starvation
was I taken from the womb
not for bombs for wounds or death

these two hands so stained and spotted
made to fondle and caress
and to gather and to give

now I seek, seek over water
under doubt and over words
in his distance beyond reach.

All the seas are rags and tatters
all the earth is made of earth
and all flesh is just a drop

but how separate are people
how unspeakably remote—
it will always be the same.

We can never prove by kissing
by embracing by our mouths
that strange love's enduring strength.

How it hurts, what pain to gather
like a body all the peace
of the world's forgotten years.

To preserve your precious silence
makes me die and gives me life
equalled by no other God.

Prudent laws and sails of windmills
golden popes and gilded words
all must pass like wind and rain.

All our crowns and all our churches
they will burn quite unsurpassed
God knows will the Chinese come.

Then a word may come to meet me
and no blessing in my mouth
but a man with whom to live.

I will eat of two words only
four can never be enough
distant love, O loving peace.

+ *For the town we live in*

Let us pray
for the town we live in
and for all our fellow citizens,
that it may become for all of us
a really human community,
a city of peace.

Let us pray
for all who live near us,
for our neighbors and acquaintances,
for our friends, and also
for those who are not well disposed toward us,
for all who surround us with affection
and also for those who give us trouble.

Let us pray
for safety in our town,
that no one's life should be endangered
by another's carelessness
and that our children may not meet with accidents.
Let us also pray
for peace and tranquillity
for all who are harrassed,
for a sound and healthy atmosphere
and an open, human climate among men.

162

Let us pray
for everyone who works here—
for our factory workers,
our artists and scholars,
our teachers and social workers
and for all who work in our hospitals
and let us also pray
for all ministers and priests
and for all who represent the Church
that they may work together
for the happiness of this town.

Let us pray
for all those who have not yet got a home of their own
and for all who are badly housed,
for those who have come here from overseas,
that they may be received with hospitality,
and for all who live alone.
We also pray for those who live in luxury and wealth,
that they may keep their homes and their hearts open
to those who are in need.

We pray
for those among us who have been struck
by illness or misfortune
or who are suffering any other trial,
for those who are bored or in anxiety or despair,
for all who have been taken away from our midst,
for those who have been sent to prison,
for the mentally ill
and for the dead and the dying.

Let us pray for ourselves,
that we may find happiness in this town
and that we do not destroy each other
by spreading hatred and division,
but that we may be,
with each other and as in one body,
the city of God on earth.

+ Lord God,
what you have sowed in us
you will reap
when your day has come
and what you have begun
here in our midst
you will complete.
We hope and expect this of you
because of Jesus,
the son of men,
whom you completed
and who, beyond our expectations,
has become our future,
living with you
today and every day.

+ You speak and call
a word that needs an answer,
a name that invites love
and gives it.
Wherever men are deaf
you are not there,
wherever men are dumb
and kill by silence
you are not among them.
Open our mouths then
and fill our hearts
with good words for each other
so that your love, your life
may be visible in us for ever.

+ *The song of the Lord in our midst*

The Lord has come to us
because he wished to stay
among his human people
and not be far away.
He is among you whom you do not know.

Although he is so near,
a man, yet God's own word,
he is not recognized
his message is not heard.
He is among you whom you do not know.

He is God's only son
born of a human mother
in every sense a man
and every man's own brother.
He is among you whom you do not know.

Show patience and forbearance
in love for his sake then
and be at one in peace
with all your fellow men.
He is among you whom you do not know.

Rejoice, I say, rejoice,
and cast away all care—
the God whom we adore
is with us everywhere.
He is among you whom you do not know.

⁺ *For the Church*

1

You called us with your voice
and made us with your word.
You brought us together,
simply people,
and we may be new people,
a new beginning of hope and peace
in this wide, uncertain world.
In your foolishness, God,
you put your name into our mouths
and your work into our hands.

2

We are your Church, a people on the way.
We have a history, a long past
of darkness and of light.
Give us now, we pray you,
a new future and call us
from the certainties, the riches
of this world in which we shelter, safely captive.
Rather make us poor and insecure,
displaced and free,
so that we may
once more hear your gospel
and follow your son.

We pray for forgiveness
for all the things that have been done
in your name in our long past—
for the violence committed by your people
in hunting heretics and in holy wars
and for the shortsightedness and pride

your Church has shown
in so many attempts to seize power.
We ask you to forgive us
because even now
your Church is not always strong enough
to refrain from violence.
Forgive us for failing
to prevent the murder of the Jews.
Forgive your Church
for so often letting down
those who are persecuted
because of their race
or the color of their skins.

4

We are not your peace in this world.
We are not your remedy and salvation
for people who are broken and divided,
because we are ourselves divided,
petty-minded and intransigent.
We betray your cause and spread confusion.
But you can give us the beginning of unity.
If we are divided into separate camps,
make us see at least
the folly of our division and be sorry for it,
so that we may no longer be content
to continue in this situation,
but think and act
in the light of your future, your promise
to make everything new,
no matter how.

Reform your Church
and give her the courage to be,
to follow you and do your word.
May she cease in her attempts
to dominate men.
May she make no more demands
and claim no more privileges,
but only try to contribute
to men's happiness.
May she neither repel nor exclude anyone
by the words she uses
or the ideas she has,
but be open to everyone
who seeks to live
a happy and creative life.
Help us to remember, God,
that we were sent
only to spread your grace
in all humility,
because we have been accepted by you
and always need forgiveness.

We remember, God,
how Jesus spoke about this world,
about you and about everything
to do with human life.
Something of what he said,
his words, his voice,
has been handed down to us—
enough to give us an idea
of who you are.
We pray that we may speak
an understandable and simple language

inspired by him.
We pray for all whose work it is
to preach the gospel
and to lead in prayer.
May they never force you on people
or wrongly use your name.
We also pray
for those who have gone out
to other lands, to sow the faith
and to serve in hardship.
And finally we pray for ourselves—
may we never run away from your silence,
but represent you as you are,
God so far and yet so near.

7

Make me serve you and others
without pushing myself forward,
so that I may help my fellow men
without humiliating them.
Make me dedicate myself
to everything that is lowly
and unimportant in the world's eyes,
so that I may do the things
that no one else takes on.
Teach me to wait, to listen
and not to speak.
Make me humble and poor enough
to accept help from others.
Send me on my way in search of food—
in search of your name.

We thank you, God,
for placing your name on our shoulders,
for giving us your gospel,
the gospel lived by Jesus Christ, the son of man,
sincerely and with all his heart.
Your word, having once passed through death,
can die no more.
It is a gleam of light
that will shine even in the distant future.
We pray
that we are not left behind,
frightened and aloof,
that we may see the new opportunities
that you offer to us—
the chance to be frankly human
at this period of history,
to be more and more fully human.
May we make what is still void
and uninhabitable
a place fit for men to live in
and what is meaningless and inhuman
bear fruit and have meaning.
Let us make a new world
where there is love and no more war.

God of Abraham
night and desert
star in the heaven
name in his flesh
seed in the dead
womb of his wife.
God of Jacob
wrestling stranger
fist that struck him
wound in his thigh.
God of Moses
burning voice, fire
under his feet
word like a cloud
pillar before him
water and bread
land of the promise.
God of David
harp in his hands
song in his mouth
love surpassing
the love of women
his house's foundation
child of his sin
cold in his bones.
God in Babel
God unspeakable
scattered abroad
God of the dead.

God of Job
man of sorrows
humiliated
lacking all form
dust a twig
weighed in the scales
of the world.
God of Jesus
shadow over
a Jewish girl
God of Auschwitz
you have blown
the ashes of Jews
over my feet.
God of me
tongue of snow
and of rapture
voice that catches
in my throat
storm-wind head-wind
covering me
tender rigid
like a body.
God of no one
simply people
march of ages
stranger we come
slowly to know
you elusive
stone of the sages
you not God

as we think you
furnace of silence
difficult friend.

+ We anticipate
what is not yet
and practice now
your future
we say and sing
that all you have made
your creation is good
laboriously
so very slowly
we work out your promise
in hope and fear
and strive to build
a city of peace
a new creation
where you will be
our light, our all.

Give us strength, O God,
to persevere
and bring us to
a happy end.